THE SEASIDE

By Jen Green

PowerKiDS press.

New York

Published in 2015 by The Rosen Publishing Group, Inc.
29 East 21st Street, New York, NY 10010

Series editor: Amy Stephenson
Series designer: Jeni Child
Crafts: Rita Storey
Craft photography: Tudor Photography
Picture researcher: Diana Morris

Picture credits:
anshar/Shutterstock: 14b. Arterra PL/Alamy: 11b Ingrid Balabanova
/Shutterstock: 10t. Joe Belanger/Shutterstock: 7t. Gordon Bell Photography
/istockphoto: 5bl. blueeyes/Shutterstock: 31t. S. Borisov/Shutterstock:
30b. Willyam Bradberry/Shutterstock: 32b. Francisco Caravana/Dreamstime:
8cl. Fred Cardoso/Shutterstock: 12t. Rich Carey/Shutterstock: 18-19 bg.
J Chambers/istockphoto: 5cl. Cultura Creative/Alamy: 26b. Ethan Daniels
/Shutterstock: 18c. Ecostock/Shutterstock: 16tr. Alex Edmonds/Shutterstock:
19bl. Jonathan Feinstein/Shutterstock: 16cl. Martin Fowler/Shutterstock:
16tc. Volodmyr Goinuk/Shutterstock: 22-23 bg. David Gomez/istockphoto:
16b. Ralf Gosch/Shutterstock: 27t. Frank Green/Shutterstock: 7b.
ImagineMedia/Shutterstock: 16tl. Gail Johnson/ Shutterstock: 24cr. Visum
Khankasens/Shutterstock: 4. Lebendkulturen.de/Shutterstock: 24bl. leoks/
Shutterstock: 28t. Lippett Photo/Shutterstock: 15t. Mana Photo/Shutterstock:
6b. Erik Mandre/Shutterstock: 23br. Maomaotou/Dreamstime: 5tr. francesco
de marco/Shutterstock: 24tl. Irina Matsiash/Shutterstock: front cover t.
V J Matthew/Shutterstock: 20b. Dave McAleavy/istockphoto: 12c. Microgen
/istockphoto: 20t. microstockman/Shutterstock: 1. Mikelane45/Dreamstime:
10b. Mike Modine/istockphoto: 22c. Nature Diver/istockphoto: 15b. Atta
Oosthuizen/Shutterstock: 11t. Pecold/Shutterstock: 6-7bg. Preto Perola
/Shutterstock: front cover c. J Prescott/istockphoto: 16cr. somchai rakin
/Shutterstock: 24cl. Rubio Photo/istockphoto: 19tr. Prillfoto/Dreamstime: 8t.
Shamleen/Shutterstock: 16c. Phillip Sharp/Alamy: 23tl. BG Smith
/Shutterstock: 8cr. Spectral Design/Shutterstock: 14-15bg. Irina Tischecko
/Shutterstock: 10-11bg. Aleksandar Todorovic/Shutterstock: 28b. viledevil/
istockphoto: 27b. Gareth Weeks /Shutterstock: 26-27bg.

Library of Congress Cataloging-in-Publication Data

Green, Jen, author.
  Projects with the seaside / by Jen Green.
     pages cm. — (Make and learn)
  Includes index.
  ISBN 978-1-4777-7173-0 (library binding) — ISBN 978-1-4777-7174-7 (pbk.) —
ISBN 978-1-4777-7175-4 (6-pack)
  1. Handicraft—Juvenile literature. 2. Seashore—Miscellanea—
Juvenile literature. 3. Shells—Miscellanea—Juvenile literature. I. Title.
  TT862.G74 2015
  745.59—dc23
                          2014014555

Manufactured in the United States of America

CPSIA Compliance Information: Batch #WS14PK9: For Further Information contact Rosen
Publishing, New York, New York at 1-800-237-9932

CONTENTS

Some of the projects in this book require scissors, paint and glue. We would recommend that children are supervised by an adult when using these things. One project also requires plaster of Paris. Children should not be allowed to handle plaster of Paris and adults handling it should always wear gloves.

! The sea can be dangerous. Make sure you have an adult with you when you visit the seaside.

AT THE SEASIDE

The seaside is the border between the land and the ocean. All sorts of plants and animals live at the seaside, and people live there, too.

The place where the land and the sea meet is called the seaside.

Scenery

Not all seaside scenery looks the same. There are many different types of coastline. There may be high cliffs, rocky **headlands** or sand **dunes**. You may find a beach covered with sand, pebbles or shells. Where a river meets the sea, there are often **mudflats**. All these places form **habitats** for different plants and animals.

QUIZ TIME!

Where else in the world do you think you might find sand dunes?

a. in a desert
b. in a forest
c. on a mountain

Answer on page 32.

Tides

Twice a day, the sea rises up the shore and then falls back again. These changes are called high **tides** and low tides. Tides are mainly caused by the pull of the Moon's **gravity** on the water. High and low tides happen at different times each day. An incoming tide can be dangerous because it can come in very quickly. If you go to the seaside, it's always good to know whether the sea is coming in or going out.

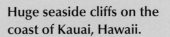
Huge seaside cliffs on the coast of Kauai, Hawaii.

Seaside records

The world's longest beach stretches for 150 miles (240 km) along the coast of Brazil in South America. The Bay of Fundy in Canada has the biggest tides. The water rises and falls more than 36 feet (11 m) here. The world's highest sea cliffs are on the islands of Hawaii in the Pacific Ocean.

At high tide the beach is covered with water.

Quick FACTS

- Different types of coasts are habitats for different plants and animals.
- Twice a day, tides rise and fall on the shore.

TRY THIS

Find photos of the same beach at high and low tide. (If you are at the seaside, you can take your own photos.) Compare the two photos. What differences can you see?

At low tide the water has gone and boats are left on the sandy beach.

ON THE BEACH

Beaches form in bays and inlets. A beach may be covered with sand, mud, pebbles, small stones or tiny shells.

! The sea can be dangerous, so make sure you have an adult with you. Never swim in the sea alone.

TRY THIS
The next time you visit the seaside, take a walk from the upper shore (p. 7) down to the water's edge. Notice features in different zones, such as the high tide mark, **shingle**, sand, rocks and rockpools. Make a map of the beach. List or draw the plants and animals you see in the different zones.

Sea power

The scenery at the coast is shaped by the sea. Waves beat at the shore every minute of every day. This wears away the land in a process called **erosion**. Some rocks at the coast are softer than others and can wear away quickly, to form a wide bay or a narrow **inlet**. The sea drops sand, shells or other materials here to form a beach.

Some of the waves that crash onto coastlines can be huge!

6

Lower shore

Middle shore

Upper shore

The three main zones on a beach.

Worn by the waves

Most of the pebbles on a beach come from nearby rocks. As waves crash against the coast, bits of rock break off. As these pieces tumble in the waves, sharp corners and jagged edges are worn away to form smooth, rounded pebbles.

Beach zones

Rising and falling tides create zones on a beach. There are three main zones: the lower, middle and upper shores. The lower shore is covered with water, except when there is a very low tide. The upper shore is dry, except at high tide. The middle shore is covered with seawater at times; the rest of the time it is dry.

? **What animals live in different zones on the beach? Turn the page to find out.**

Seaweed left at the high tide mark on a beach.

Beach habitats

Each zone on the beach is home to its own set of plants and animals. Animals of the upper shore include small, shrimp-like sandhoppers, which lurk among seaweed that has been left at the high tide mark. Crabs hide in the sand and among rocks on the middle shore. Sea anemones (p. 15) and starfish live in tide pools on the lower shore.

A starfish clings to an underwater rock.

A tide pool on the lower shore.

QUIZ TIME!

Which of these animals might you find by the sea?

   a. cat
   b. dog whelk
   c. squirrel

Answer on page 32.

Quick *FACTS*

• Beaches form where pebbles, stones or sand build up in a bay or inlet.
• The upper, middle and lower shores are home to many different plants and animals.

Make This

Shells and other things you find on a beach are great for craft projects. You could make a beach hut mirror to hang in your bathroom or bedroom.

You could use driftwood to make this into a photo frame instead. Or you could make a mirror that looks like a tide pool.

1 Cut a large rectangle of foam board as big as you want the finished hut to be. Glue strips of blue paper onto the foam board as shown.

2 Trim the sides and along the roof to make the shape of your beach hut.

3 Place a small rectangular mirror in the centre of your hut and draw around it. Ask an adult to carefully cut out the shape to make a rectangular hole.

4 Tape a piece of card stock over the hole on the back of your hut. Glue the mirror inside the hole and onto the card stock so the mirror side is facing out.

5 Glue sand and shells onto the foam board at the bottom of the beach hut. Tape a piece of string onto the back so you can hang up your mirror.

TIP: You can also buy shells from craft shops if you haven't visited a beach.

IN THE SAND

Sandy beaches are full of life, but most of it is hidden. Many animals live in burrows in the sand.

Wet sand has been made into a sandcastle on a beach.

What is sand?

Sand is made of tiny grains of rock and shell that have been smashed up by the waves and then dropped onto the shore. Just one square metre of beach contains millions of these grains. Sand is an amazing material. Dry sand runs through your fingers, but when it is wet, sand sticks together, so you can use it to build sandcastles.

Empty razor clam shells. Razor clams live in burrows in the sand.

A crab comes out of its sandy burrow. Crabs are scavengers – they eat anything they can find.

Crabs

You will often see crabs on a beach. Some types live in burrows in the sand. Others live in rockpools. Crabs have eight legs. They also have a pair of claws that can pinch you if you're not careful. Crabs belong to a group of animals called **crustaceans**. This group includes shrimp and lobsters. They all have a hard body case or shell.

Buried in the sand

Two main groups of animals live in the sand: clams such as razor clams and worms, such as ragworms and lugworms. Lugworms swallow sand and **filter** out tiny bits of food. Razor clams are also filter-feeders. Ragworms are **predators**. At high tide they come to the surface to look for **prey**, such as lugworms.

TRY THIS

Lugworms live in U-shaped burrows. At the head end is a little pit, made by the worm as it swallows sand. The waste sand comes out its other end, to leave a little worm-shaped cast at the surface. Look for these lugworm casts on the beach.

TIP: If you can't visit a beach you can see similar casts in soil that have been made by earthworms.

? What leaves tracks in the sand? Turn the page to find out.

The collared plover is a type of shorebird.

Making tracks

Seabirds, crabs and other animals leave tracks on a sandy beach. Become a beach detective. Study the prints and try to identify the animals that made them. Each type of bird leaves different tracks. For example, gulls have **webbed** feet. Shorebirds such as turnstones have long, narrow toes. See if you can follow the tracks to find out where the animals went.

Shorebirds have left tracks in the sand with their feet.

TIP: If you don't live by a beach you could follow tracks in mud that have been made by birds and animals in a wood or garden.

Quick *FACTS*

- Sand is made of tiny grains of smashed up rock or shell.
- Many animals found on beaches live under the sand in burrows.

QUIZ TIME!

Most beaches have yellow or brown sand, but where can you find a beach with purple sand?

a. **Australia**

b. **Italy**

c. **the USA**

Answer on page 32.

Make This

Just like animal and bird tracks, shells and other objects pressed into sand leave marks too. You can make a paperweight by using sand to help you make a cast of a seashell.

> ! Plaster of Paris should only be handled by an adult.

You could make casts of other seaside objects, such as driftwood, for a seaside-themed display. Try painting them to look like real pieces of wood.

1 Fill a large plastic tub with sand. Mix it with water until the sand is damp, but not too wet.

2 Press the patterned side of some seashells firmly into the sand.

3 Gently remove the seashells. They should leave an impression in the sand. If the impression caves in when you take the shells out, your sand is either too wet or too dry. You will need to try again!

4 Ask an adult to mix up some plaster of Paris and carefully spoon the mixture into the shapes on the sand. (Gloves must be worn when doing this, and remember to wash the spoon!) Leave the mix to set. This will take a few days.

5 When the plaster has dried completely, lift out the shell shapes and brush off any sand. Paint the plaster shells with glue and cover them with glitter. Let dry.

IN A TIDE POOL

Tide pools appear on rocky coasts when the tide has gone out. They are incredibly rich in wildlife, including small fish, shrimps, sea anemones and shellfish.

All change

Animals that live in tide pools have to cope with changing conditions. As the tide comes in, waves crash into the pool, and swirling seawater fills it. At low tide the pool shrinks as the water drains back out. Tide pool creatures are specially **adapted** to survive in this changing environment.

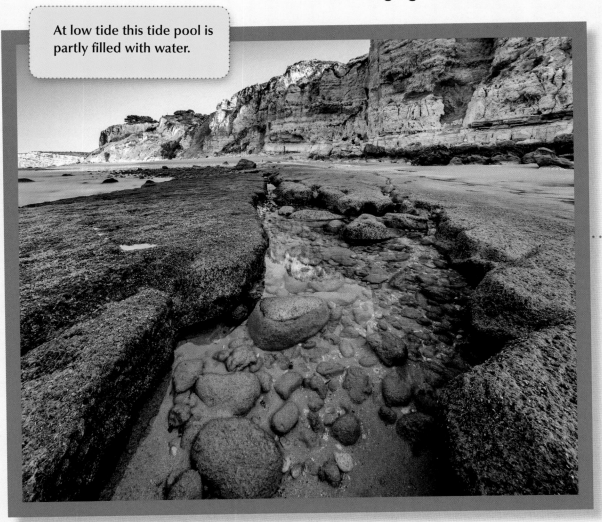

At low tide this tide pool is partly filled with water.

Limpets have a very strong grip, which means they can cling onto seaside rocks.

Holding on!

Limpets and barnacles are shelled creatures that live in tide pools and on rocky shores. They cling onto rocks using the wide foot on their underside. Their grip on the rock is very strong! At high tide, barnacles filter tiny bits of food from the water with their hairy legs.

TRY THIS

Have you ever tried to pick a limpet off a rock? They might seem to be stuck there, but in fact they move about to feed on tiny plants that grow on the rocks. Put a blob of model paint on some limpet shells. Make a map of their exact positions. Go back the next day to see if the limpets have moved. You could also use the same method to track garden snails.

Sea anemones

At low tide sea anemones look like blobs of jelly on the rocks. But at high tide they open up and spread their stinging **tentacles**. They look like plants but they are actually animals. Any small creatures that come within reach are captured by the tentacles and dragged into the sea anemone's mouth.

A sea anemone's mouth is surrounded by its stinging tentacles.

? What animals live in the shells you find on beaches? Turn the page to find out.

Periwinkles

Whelk

Topshell

Shells and shellfish

Shellfish are soft-bodied animals that live inside a hard shell. The main group are **mollusks**, which are related to garden snails. Mollusks such as whelks, periwinkles and topshells have a single shell with a spiral shape. Scallops, cockles and mussels have two shells joined by a little hinge.

Scallop

Cockles

Mussels

Quick *FACTS*

- Tide pools are home to animals such as shrimp, starfish, mollusks and sea anemones.
- These creatures have to cope with changing conditions as tides rise and fall.

QUIZ TIME!

Which of these crabs is the smallest?

a. blue crab

b. pea crab

c. spider crab

Answer on page 32.

Make This

Seashells come in many different shapes and colors. You can create a seashell wind chime using the shells you find on a beach.

Shells come in many shapes and sizes because different animals live in them. What can you find out about the animals that lived in your wind chime shells?

TIP: You can also buy shells from craft shops if you haven't visited a beach.

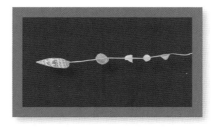

! You will need strong glue or a hot glue gun to do this – ask an adult to help you.

1

Cut four pieces of string, each piece about 1 foot (30 cm) long. It doesn't matter if they aren't exactly the same length. Place shells along the length of each string. When you are happy, glue them in place.

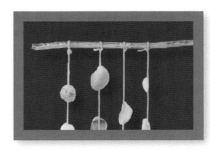

2

When the glue has dried, tie one end of each string onto a twig.

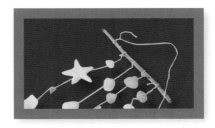

3

Cut another length of string. Tie the ends of the string onto each end of the twig.

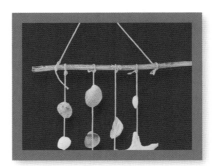

4

Hang the seashell wind chime in a breezy place, such as a window. The shells will clink together to create the wind chime effect.

IN THE WATER

Other wildlife, such as fish, seals and dolphins live in the sea. Seaweed also grows here.

This type of seaweed, which grows in deep water, is called kelp.

Seawater and seaweed

Seawater tastes salty because it is full of salt, which **dissolves** in it. Everything that lives in the sea is adapted to a saltwater habitat.

Seaweeds belong to a group of plants called algae. Many types can be found on the shore or in shallow water. Some types, such as kelp, grow in deep water. All seaweeds fix themselves to underwater rocks using a root-like part called a holdfast. They grow upwards towards the sunlight, which they need to make their food and grow.

Seals spend most of their time in the water, but sometimes come ashore.

Life underwater

Fish, crabs and starfish live among the seaweed. It is safer for them there as they can hide from predators. They also lay their eggs there to help keep them safe. Like all animals, they breathe **oxygen**, but they don't come to the surface to get it. Instead they **absorb** oxygen from the water using feathery structures called **gills**.

Marine mammals

Coastal waters are home to **mammals** such as seals and dolphins. Seals come ashore to **bask** on rocks in the sunshine and to give birth. Dolphins live in the water all of the time. They are naturally curious and sometimes follow boats. Like all mammals they cannot breathe underwater. They come to the surface of the water to breathe air.

Smaller sea creatures, such as these kelp bass, feel safer swimming among the seaweed.

QUIZ TIME!

Which of these animals can't breathe underwater?

a. octopus

b. whale

c. shark

Answer on page 32.

? Which fish hide on the seafloor? Turn the page to find out.

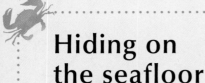

Hiding on the seafloor

If you stand in the shallows and look down, you may be lucky enough to spot a flatfish, such as a plaice. These flattened fish rest on the seafloor. The colors and patterns on their bodies exactly match the seafloor. This **camouflage** makes them very hard to find.

The dots and patches on this plaice's body help it to camouflage itself against the seafloor.

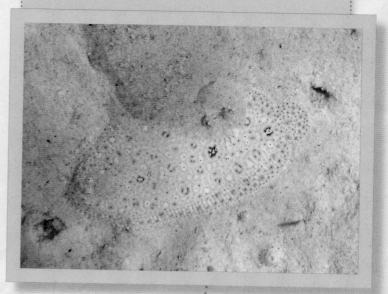

Beachcombers find all kinds of things on a beach, such as old fishing nets and shells.

TRY THIS

Things from the sea can wash up on beaches. Items you find on the shore give clues about the plants and animals that live in the water. Become a **beachcomber**. Look for shells, egg cases and crab claws among the seaweed. You may find jellyfish, starfish and sea urchins washed up on the beach.

Quick *FACTS*

- Fish, starfish and seaweeds live in the waters off the coast.
- Flatfish, such as plaice, use camouflage to hide on the seafloor.

Make This

Seaweed grows in beautiful shapes. Make seaweed pictures using a blown paint technique. You could use it to make a seaweed background for an underwater scene.

These blown paintings look great grouped together in different colors. You can also use the same technique to create plants, such as trees and shrubs.

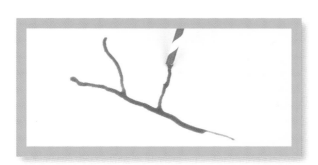

1 Water down some poster or watercolor paint so that it is runny. Dip the end of a straw into the paint and use the straw to draw the basic shape of your seaweed.

2 Use the end of the straw to draw thinner branches sprouting from the main branches as shown. (You could use a picture of some seaweed to help you decide what shape your seaweed should be.)

3 Before the paint dries, gently blow the it through the other end of the straw. The paint on the paper will fan out and make lovely shapes that look like seaweed. Let dry.

ON THE CLIFFS

Cliffs form at the coast where hills made of hard rock line the ocean. Cliffs provide homes for plants, insects, spiders and nesting birds.

The sea has worn a deep groove into these cliffs. There is now a beach where part of the cliff was.

Crumbling cliffs

Cliff coastlines are constantly changing as the edge of the land is worn away by the sea. As waves crash against the base of the cliffs, they wear a groove. The groove gets deeper and deeper, and finally the rocks on top collapse. Crumbling cliffs are dangerous, so never go too close to the edge.

QUIZ TIME!

Which of these birds like to nest on sea cliffs?

a. blackbirds
b. robins
c. terns

Answer on page 32.

Seaside plants

Clifftops are breezy places. They are home to plants that don't mind the salty air or the strong winds blowing off the ocean. These tough plants include gorse and heather. Thrift and campion grow close to the ground, out of the wind. Their flowers attract insects such as bees and butterflies, and also spiders that prey on insects.

Insects such as butterflies visit seaside flowers to drink nectar.

Puffins like to perch on steep cliffs. This helps the birds to keep away from any predators.

Nesting birds

Steep cliffs may be dangerous for people, but they are great places to rear your young if you can fly. Seabirds, such as puffins, nest in **colonies** on narrow ledges, where their eggs and young are safe from most predators. Puffins and gannets dive into the ocean to catch fish for their young.

? What is a seaside food chain? Turn the page to find out.

Gannet

Seaside food chains

Seaside animals eat plants or other animals. In turn, they may be eaten by larger predators. Diagrams called food chains show who eats what. Gannets feed on fish called mackerel, which feed on tiny shrimp-like crustaceans, such as **copepods**. The gannet, mackerel and shrimp form a simple food chain.

Mackerel

Mackerel

★ TRY THIS

Seabirds such as gannets dive into the sea to catch fish such as mackerel. Other birds fish from the surface. Use binoculars to spot seabirds fishing. Binoculars are also useful for watching birds anywhere.

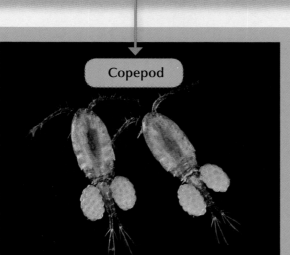

Copepod

Quick *FACTS*

- Cliffs form habitats for wildlife, such as plants, insects, spiders and seabirds.
- Wave erosion causes cliffs to crumble.
- Many seabirds live in colonies.

Make This

Food chain mobiles are a great way to show who eats what at the seaside. This mobile shows the food chain of a puffin, which hunts sand eels. Sand eels feed on smaller fish.

You can make food chains for animals that live in all kinds of habitats. Or you could make the puffin food chain longer by adding in what the small fish eat. Do you think puffins are eaten by any other animals?

1 Draw a puffin on a piece of paper. You could trace this one or you can copy one from a book or from the Internet.

2 Cut out your puffin. Paint or color it in and then glue it onto a circle of colored card stock.

3 Cut out a few long sand eel shapes from silver foil. Glue them onto a circle of colored card stock. Cut out some tiny fish shapes and glue them onto another circle of colored card stock.

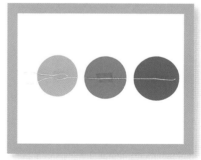

4 Lay your circles face down in a line. Make sure you get the order of your food chain right! Tape a length of string onto the back and tape a loop at the top to hang up your food chain.

LIVING AT THE SEASIDE

Coasts are popular places to live and to visit. People use the sea for food, minerals, energy and transportation. About one in every five people in the world lives by the sea.

Food from the sea

The sea is an important source of food such as fish, crabs, shrimps and lobsters. Some types of seaweed are also eaten and sea salt is used to flavor food.

People have gathered food from the sea since **prehistoric** times. Seaside villages and towns often grow up around natural harbors that offer shelter for fishing boats.

Fishermen working on board their boat.

Minerals and energy

The sea is also a valuable source of **minerals**. Gold, silver and copper are mined from the seafloor. A type of gem called a pearl forms inside the shells of a type of mollusc, called an oyster.

Oil and natural gases are sometimes drilled from the seafloor of coastal waters. Seashores also help make energy. The power from wind, waves and tides can be used to make electricity.

Transport and trade

For hundreds of years the sea has been used as a highway, to move goods and people around the coast or across the sea to faraway places. Small fishing villages grew into ports, and then busy towns and cities that became centres for trade and industry. The sea is still the cheapest way of transporting goods between countries.

Giant cranes unload cargo from a ship at a busy port.

QUIZ TIME!

Pearls are found inside oysters, but what is inside a natural pearl?

   a. a tiny animal

   b. a grain of sand

   c. nothing

Answer on page 32.

? Can you think of any other ways people use the seaside? Turn the page to find out.

Tourism

The seaside is a very popular place to visit. About 60 years ago, cheap air travel arrived and people began to go abroad for their vacations. Now tourism is big business in many countries. Whether at home or abroad, the seaside is a great place to swim, relax and explore, or just enjoy the scenery. Coastlines all over the world are now popular **resorts**.

A beach at a resort in Palawn, Philippines.

Tourists enjoy the sunshine, sand and sea at a beach in Romania.

Quick *FACTS*

- The seaside is a popular place to live and visit.
- The sea provides food, minerals, energy and a means of transportation.
- Many people go to the seaside for their vacations.

TRY THIS

Research a resort and make a list of what goes on there. Are boats in the harbor used for fishing, mining, trade or transportation? Does tourism provide jobs for sailors, tour guides and people working in cafés, restaurants and shops? Make a poster showing what your resort has to offer.

Make this

Stencils are a great way of using simple patterns to build up a picture. You can make your own seaside themed cards and envelopes.

You can make all sorts of other amazing things using stencils. Simple starfish and shell shapes would make a funky design for wrapping paper, or some party invitations!

1 Draw a simple outline of a picture, such as a sailboat and some seabirds.

2 Ask an adult to cut out the middle of your design with a craft knife.

3 Tape the stencil onto whatever you want to decorate, such as a card and an envelope. Load your paintbrush with some paint and then dab off any excess on a scrap of paper. Dab the paint through the stencil. Remove the stencil and then let the paint dry.

4 You can repeat your design as many time as you like and you can also try using different colors, too.

GLOSSARY

absorb to take in

adapted suitable for something

bask to lie in the sun

beachcomber a person who looks for things on a beach

camouflage colors and patterns on an animal's body that help it blend in with its surroundings

colonies large groups of animals, such as seabirds, which live close together

copepods tiny shrimp-like crustaceans that are food for fish such as mackerel

crustaceans a group of (usually) marine animals with a hard body case

dissolves when a solid becomes part of a liquid

dunes mounds of sand

erosion when the land is worn away by natural forces, such as water

filter to remove small bits

gills the feathery parts on fish and other sea animals, which are used to absorb oxygen from the water

gravity the force that pulls one object towards another

habitat natural home of plants and animals

headlands rocky areas that jut out into the sea

inlet a bay or a narrow passage of water on the coast

mammals animals that have hair and feed their young milk

mined dug from the ground

mineral a natural non-living substance

mollusc a type of animal with a soft body, such as a slug, a snail or a limpet

mudflats muddy banks, often at the mouth of a river (where the river meets the sea)

oxygen gas in the air that living things need to breathe

predators animals that hunt other animals for food

prehistoric the time before written records were made

prey animals that are hunted for food

resorts places people visit on vacation, often on beaches

shingle small stones on a beach

tentacles long feelers, often covered with stinging needles. Used by sea creatures to capture their food

tides the rise and fall in sea levels on the coast

webbed the skin between an animal's toes, which make its feet work like paddles

BOOKS

Beaches
by Emma Carlson Berne
(PowerKids Press, 2008)

Beaches
by JoAnn Early Macken (Gareth Stevens
Publishing, 2006)

Geographywise: Coasts
by Jen Green (Wayland Books, 2012)

History Snapshots: The Seaside
by Sarah Ridley (Franklin Watts, 2011)

Nature Trail: Seaside
By Jen Green (Wayland Books, 2010)

A Walk From: Our Seaside School
by Deborah Chancellor (Franklin Watts, 2014)

WEBSITES

Due to the changing nature of Internet links, PowerKids Press has developed an online list of websites related to the subject of this book. This site is updated regularly. Please use this link to access the list: www.powerkidslinks.com/mal/sea/

INDEX

QUIZ ANSWERS

Page 4: **a** – in a desert. The biggest sand dunes in the world are in the Sahara desert.

Page 8: **a** – a dog whelk

Page 12: c – in the USA (Pfeiffer Beach, California)

Page 16: a – pea crab

Page 19: b – a whale

Page 22: c – terns

Page 27: b – a tiny animal (which gets trapped inside an oyster's shell)